An Alphabet of Colors

By Sarah McPherson

To Jamie
Thanks for letting me see the world
through your eyes.

Colors of the Alphabet

Written by Sarah McPherson

Copyright © Tarva Publishing

All rights reserved. No part of this book may be reproduced in any manner whatsoever without prior written permission of the publisher.

First Printing, 2022

Published by Tarva Publishing
www.tarvapublishing.com.au

ISBN 978-0-6454689-0-8

There are many colors of the
Alphabet
in that we do agree,

From   , Amazon and Amber
to colors like Zaffre

So can you see your favorite
with the A-Z of color

Or if you had made this book
would you choose another?

A

Amazon

B

Blue

C

cyan

D

Dark Orange

E

Emerald

F

Flame

G

Green

H

Helioptrope

I

Imperial Red

J

Jade

K

Kobe

L

Lilac

M

Mango

N

Nickel

O

Orange

P

Pear

Quicksilver

R

Red

S

Saffron

T

Teal

u

unmellow yellow

V

volt

W

wisteria

X

xanthic

Y

Yale Blue

Z

Zomp

So did you see your favorite color in our book?

Head back to the start and take another look!

Red, orange, yellow, green, blue, purple, pink, grey, brown, black, indigo, violet,

www.ingramcontent.com/pod-product-compliance
Lightning Source LLC
Chambersburg PA
CBHW040729020526
44107CB00086B/2988